First Facts®

Snakes

Garter Snakes

by Van Wallach

Consultant:
Robert T. Mason, PhD
Professor of Zoology
J.C. Braly Curator of Vertebrates
Oregon State University, Corvallis

Capstone
press®

Mankato, Minnesota

First Facts is published by Capstone Press,
151 Good Counsel Drive, P.O. Box 669, Mankato, Minnesota 56002.
www.capstonepress.com

Library of Congress Cataloging-in-Publication Data
Wallach, V. (Van)
    Garter snakes / by Van Wallach.
    p. cm. — (First facts. Snakes)
    Includes bibliographical references and index.
    Summary: "A brief introduction to garter snakes, including their habitat, food,
and life cycle." — Provided by publisher.
    ISBN-13: 978-1-4296-1924-0 (hardcover)
    ISBN-10: 1-4296-1924-4 (hardcover)
    1. Garter snakes — Juvenile literature. I. Title. II. Series.
QL666.O636W35 2009
597.96'2 — dc22   2007051904

Editorial Credits

Lori Shores, editor; Ted Williams, designer and illustrator; Danielle Ceminsky,
    illustrator; Jo Miller, photo researcher

Photo Credits

Alamy/Randall Ingalls, 7; Rick & Nora Bowers, 9
BigStockPhoto.com/Steve Byland, 13
Getty Images Inc./National Geographic/Norbert Rosing, 10–11
iStockphoto/John Rich, 17
Nature Picture Library/Martin Dohrn, 21; Todd Pusser, 18
Pete Carmichael, 12, 15
Peter Arnold/James Gerholdt, 1, cover
Shutterstock/Cathy Keifer, 5; Nahimoff, background texture (throughout)
Tom Stack & Associates, Inc./Joe McDonald, 8
Visuals Unlimited/G. & C. Merker, 20

Essential content terms are **bold** and are defined at the bottom of the page where they first appear.

1 2 3 4 5 6 13 12 11 10 09 08

Table of Contents

A Striped Snake

Have you ever seen a snake in your backyard? Chances are it was a little garter snake. These harmless reptiles are only about 2 to 3 feet (61 to 91 centimeters) long.

Like all snakes, garter snakes' bodies are covered with **scales**. Most garter snakes are brown or black. They have yellow, white, orange, or red stripes. Some garter snakes are spotted.

scales: small pieces of hard, dry skin

Far and Wide

Garter snakes live almost everywhere in the United States and Mexico. They are the most common snake in North America.

Garter Snake Range

where garter snakes live

North America

Europe

Asia

Africa

South America

Australia

Antarctica

N
W E
S

6

Garter snakes live below sea level in Death Valley, California. They have also been found high up in the mountains of Mexico.

Wet and Grassy Homes

Garter snakes usually live near water. They can swim much faster than they crawl. Garter snakes dive into water and swim away to escape danger.

Garter snakes also live in gardens and grassy areas. They lie in the sun to get warm. All snakes are **cold-blooded**. Their body temperature changes with the air and ground around them.

cold-blooded: having a body temperature that matches the surroundings

A Winter Nap

Snakes **hibernate** when the weather gets cold. In the winter, garter snakes gather together in underground **dens**.

Some snakes wander miles away from their winter dens in the summer. But these snakes find their way back. Garter snakes return to the same den every year.

Fun Fact!
A snake's winter den is called a hibernaculum.

den: a sheltered area where snakes hibernate
hibernate: to spend winter in a resting state

On the Hunt

Garter snakes hunt during the day. In the water, they use their eyesight to find fish. On land, they use their sense of smell to find small **prey** like frogs.

prey: an animal hunted by another animal for food

Fun Fact!
Garter snakes swallow their prey while it is still alive.

Snake tongues do more than just taste. Snakes pick up scents from the air with their forked tongues. A special organ in the roof of their mouths identifies tastes and smells.

Growing Up

Garter snakes mate once each year. The female releases a scent to attract males. Some garter snakes form a mating ball. This happens when many males try to mate with one female.

Some snakes lay eggs, but not the garter snake. Female garter snakes give birth to live baby snakes. The newborn snakes are only about 5 to 10 inches (13 to 25 centimeters) long at birth.

Fun Fact!
Newborn snakes do not eat until after they shed their skin for the first time. Usually this happens 7 to 10 days after birth.

Life Cycle of a Garter Snake

Newborn
Between 10 and 40 snakes are born at one time.

Young
Young snakes take two to three years to reach adulthood.

Newborn

Adult
Male and female garter snakes mate in the spring.

Danger

Garter snakes have many **predators**. Water birds, hawks, and owls eat snakes. Raccoons and foxes catch and eat snakes too.

Garter snakes live closer to humans than most other snakes. Sometimes people and household pets such as cats kill garter snakes.

predator: an animal that hunts other animals for food

scales

tail

18

A Stinky Defense

Garter snakes try to escape if they sense danger. But if they are caught off-guard, they have a smelly way to defend themselves. Garter snakes produce a stinky liquid called musk. When in danger, they squirt the liquid from glands near the tail. The musk also tastes very bad. An animal will spit out a garter snake when it tastes the musk.

Fun Fact!
Musk smells so strong that you cannot wash it off for several days.

19

Long Life

Garter snakes live about 10 to 15 years. They may live longer when kept as pets or in zoos. One garter snake lived in a zoo for 22 years.

Fun Fact!
Common garter snakes can survive being frozen for three hours!

Amazing but True!

The largest known snake den is near Winnipeg, Canada. People come from all over to see it. Scientists study the snakes that return year after year. More than 75,000 red-sided garter snakes hibernate there. It must get crowded in the winter!

Glossary

cold-blooded (KOLD-BLUH-id) — having a body temperature that changes with the surroundings

den (DEHN) — a shelter where a wild animal may live; snakes only use dens to hibernate in the winter

hibernate (HYE-bur-nate) — to spend winter in a resting state as if in a deep sleep

predator (PREH-duh-tor) — an animal that hunts other animals for food

prey (PRAY) — an animal hunted by another animal for food

scale (SKALE) — one of the small pieces of hard skin that cover the body of a reptile

Read More

Doeden, Matt. *Garter Snakes.* World of Reptiles. Mankato, Minn.: Capstone Press, 2005.

McDonald, Mary Ann. *Garter Snakes.* New Naturebooks. Chanhassen, Minn.: The Child's World, 2007.

Silverman, Buffy. *Gliding Garter Snakes.* Pull Ahead Books. Minneapolis: Lerner, 2007.

Internet Sites

FactHound offers a safe, fun way to find Internet sites related to this book. All of the sites on FactHound have been researched by our staff.

Here's how:
1. Visit *www.facthound.com*
2. Choose your grade level.
3. Type in this book ID **1429619244** for age-appropriate sites. You may also browse subjects by clicking on letters, or by clicking on pictures and words.
4. Click on the **Fetch It** button.

FactHound will fetch the best sites for you!

Index